Kingfisher Books, Grisewood & Dempsey Ltd,
Elsley House, 24-30 Great Titchfield Street,
London W1P 7AD

First published in 1993 by Kingfisher Books
2 4 6 8 10 9 7 5 3

Material in this edition was previously published by
Kingfisher Books in *On the Move: Jumbo Jet* in 1990.

© Grisewood & Dempsey Ltd 1990, 1993

Series editor: Veronica Pennycook
Series designer: Terry Woodley
Cover illustration by Jane Gedye/Young Artists
Typeset in 3B2
Phototypeset by SPAN
Printed in Great Britain by
BPCC Paulton Books Limited

The Jumbo Jet

Angela Royston
Illustrated by George Buchanan

Kingfisher Books

In this book

This book is all about a jumbo jet. The type of jet in this story is a Boeing 747.

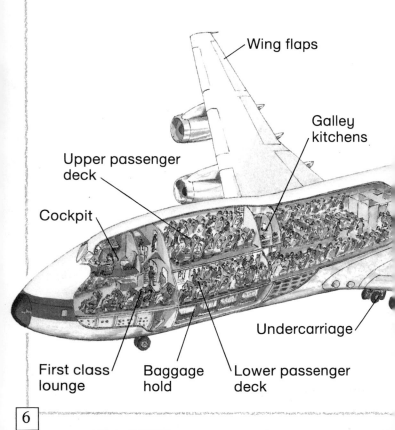

Wing flaps

Galley kitchens

Upper passenger deck

Cockpit

Undercarriage

First class lounge

Baggage hold

Lower passenger deck

The Boeing 747 is one of the biggest passenger aircraft and it can carry over 400 passengers. Boeing 747s can fly for very long distances without having to stop for more fuel.

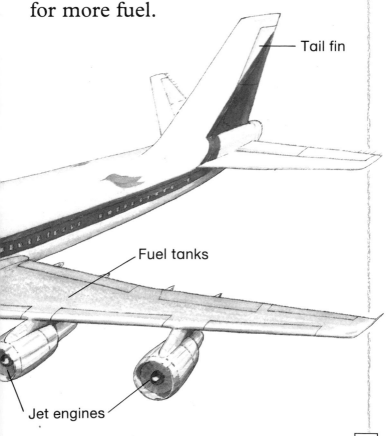

Tail fin

Fuel tanks

Jet engines

Cleared for take-off

It is morning at a busy airport in New York. Lots of planes are taking off and landing. Tom, the pilot of a jumbo jet, steers the jet to the end of the runway. Then he waits for permission to take-off.

At last the message comes from the control tower: "Bluebird 202 cleared for take-off." Tom pushes the throttle forward and the jet engines roar as they build up power. The jumbo jet starts to speed down the runway.

Into the air

Tom pulls the control column and the heavy plane rises into the air. Then he moves a lever to pull up the plane's wheels.

As the plane climbs higher and higher, some passengers look out of the windows.

Soon the airport has been left far behind and New York's tall skyscapers look like matchboxes. The jumbo jet climbs through the clouds and into the sunshine. It is on its way to London.

Avoiding the storm

Air Traffic Control at New York
tells Kate, the co-pilot, how high
to fly and which route to take.
She quickly taps this information
into the plane's computer. Now
Tom switches over to automatic
pilot so the plane will fly itself.

Tom, Kate and John, the
engineer, watch the dials to make
sure everything is working well.

Kate spots a dark blob on the
weather radar. She warns Tom
and he puts a new route into the
computer to avoid the storm.

Serving a meal

Meanwhile, the passengers settle
down for the long journey ahead.
It will take the jumbo jet nearly
seven hours to fly to London.

In the galley, Maria and the rest
of the cabin crew heat up a meal
for everyone.

Maria loads the trays of food on to a trolley and sets off down the aisle. As she hands a meal to one boy he says, "Just look at those black clouds."

"Yes," she replies, "there's a big thunderstorm going on over there, but we're going round it."

Engine trouble

The plane has been flying for five hours when John notices that one of the dials has lit up. He checks the other dials and then tells Tom, "Engine number three is overheating."

Tom takes that engine off automatic control. He makes it work more slowly so it cools down. "I'll report it to the ground crew when we land," he says.

The jumbo jet flies on as the Sun begins to set. They will soon reach London airport.

Ready to land

When the plane begins to fly
down, Maria checks that the
passengers have fastened their
seat belts. Radio instruments
guide Tom and show him how
high the plane should be.

The plane gets lower and lower. Soon the crew can see the runway lights. Tom lowers the flaps on the wings to slow the plane down.

"Bluebird 202 cleared to land," radios the control tower. Tom lowers the wheels and a few seconds later the plane lands.

At the airport

The plane rushes down the runway, and Tom quickly uses the brakes and engines to slow it down.

He steers the jumbo jet to the passenger buildings, where he brings the plane to a stop.

Jetties are joined to the side of the plane so the passengers can walk into the airport terminal.

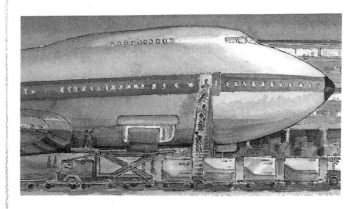

Trolleys soon arrive beside the baggage hold and the passengers' suitcases are loaded into them and taken inside the airport.

As the crew are going off the plane to rest, the cleaners arrive to start work. They will tidy and clean the inside of the plane.

Outside, a petrol wagon has pulled up. The driver connects a long hose to the plane's fuel tanks. The jet is filled up with petrol that comes straight from a huge tank beneath the airport.

Mending the engine

Tom tells Lee, the ground engineer, about the problem with engine number three. "I'll look at it right away," says Lee, as he picks up his tool box.

Lee and another engineer are raised up to the engine. They lift the engine cover and prop it open. Lee looks inside using some special instruments. "We'll have to change this engine tonight," he says.

The next flight

It's just getting light when the jumbo jet is ready to fly again. A new crew arrives and checks that everything is ready.

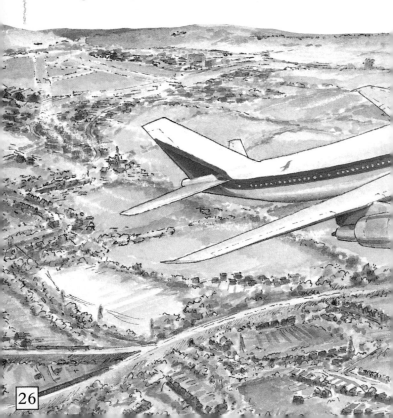

The passengers and luggage come on board and the doors close. Then the pilot steers the plane to the runway. He lowers the wing flaps so the plane will lift into the air. They are cleared for take-off. Next stop Jamaica!

Some special words

Air Traffic Control People who control where and when aircraft fly.

Control column A lever which makes a plane fly higher or lower.

Control tower A building at an airport with computers, radar and people working in Air Traffic Control.

Jetty A passageway through which passengers walk on and off the plane.

Radar An instrument which detects large objects and shows them on a screen.

Throttle A lever which increases or decreases the power of the engines.

Index

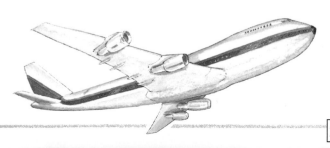